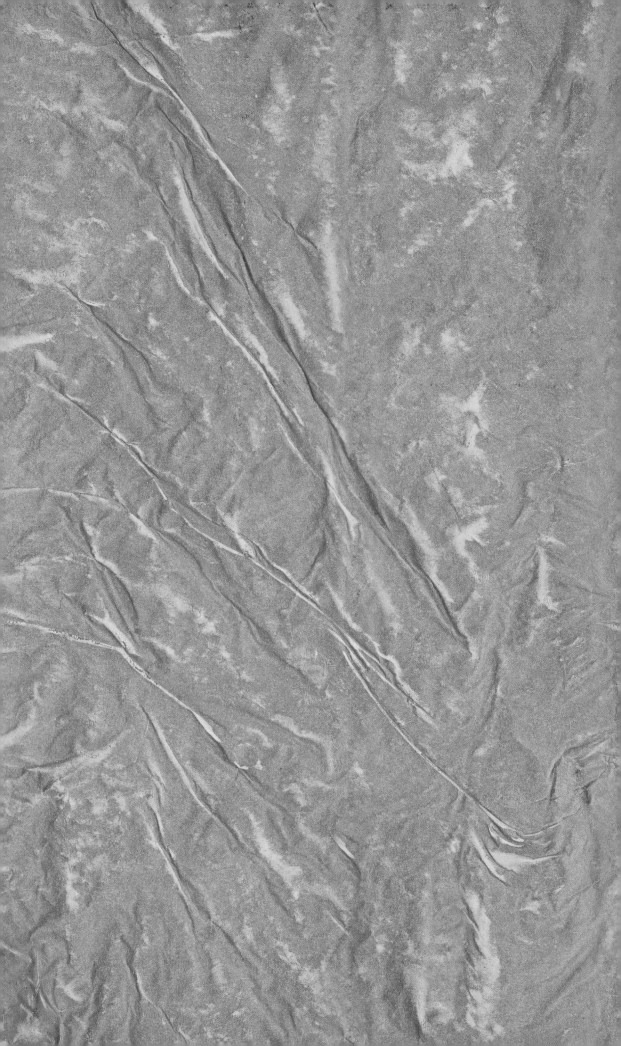

Rain Play

Cynthia Cotten

Illustrated by Javaka Steptoe

HENRY HOLT AND COMPANY
NEW YORK

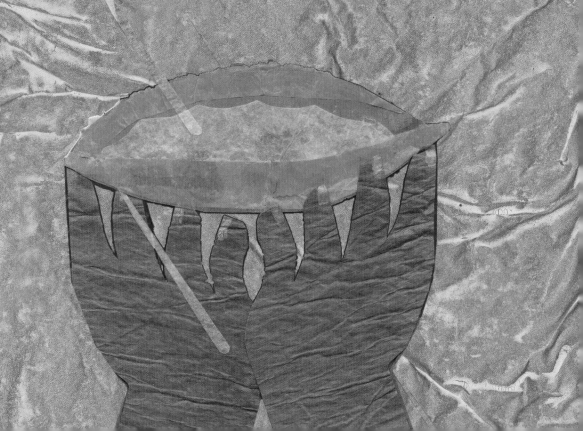

Henry Holt and Company, LLC
Publishers since 1866
175 Fifth Avenue
New York, New York 10010
www.HenryHoltKids.com

Henry Holt ® is a registered trademark of Henry Holt and Company, LLC.
Text copyright © 2008 by Cynthia Cotten
Illustrations copyright © 2008 by Javaka Steptoe
Distributed in Canada by H. B. Fenn and Company Ltd.

Library of Congress Cataloging-in-Publication Data
Cotten, Cynthia.
Rain play / Cynthia Cotten ; illustrated by Javaka Steptoe.—1st ed.
p.   cm.
Summary: Most people leave the park when rain begins to fall, while others enjoy the
sights, sounds, and feel of the cool water—until thunder and lightning come near.
ISBN-13: 978-0-8050-6795-8 / ISBN-10: 0-8050-6795-7
[1. Rain and rainfall—Fiction. 2. Play—Fiction. 3. Parks—Fiction.
4. Thunderstorms—Fiction. 5. Stories in rhyme.] I. Steptoe, Javaka, ill. II. Title.
PZ8.3.C8284Rai 2008   [E]—dc22   2007012734

First Edition—2008 / Designed by Amelia May Anderson and Barbara Grzeslo
The artist used cut-paper collage and paint to create the illustrations in this book.
Printed in the United States of America on acid-free paper. ∞
1 3 5 7 9 10 8 6 4 2

For Andrea Perry and Dave Crawley,
my forever partners in rhyme
—C. C.

When was the last time
you did cartwheels till you were dizzy,
then ran as fast as you could,
racing fireflies, laughing?
—J. S.

At the park
the sky grows dark.

See the breeze
toss the trees.

Plip, plop.
Drip, drop.

Rain begins.
Cools our skins.

Raindrops splatter.
People scatter.

But we stay
    awhile and play

Tippy-toe as puddles grow.

I'm a flower
in a shower.

Splashing,
splishing.

Look! We're fishing.

Make a boat.
Watch it float.

A leaf's a cup.
Fill it up.

Running, romping, puddle-stomping.

Here we are,
in the car.

Wipers swish.
Sneakers squish.

Home once more.
In the door.

Snug inside,
warmed and dried.

Watch the drops
until it stops.

There's the sun.

The
rain
is
done!

5